GOLDEN GATE BRIDGE

Published by Creative Education
123 South Broad Street
Mankato, Minnesota 56001

Creative Education is an imprint of The Creative Company.

Designed by Stephanie Blumenthal
Production design by Melinda Belter
Art direction by Rita Marshall

Photographs by Alamy (Wm. Baker / GhostWorx Images, Gary Crabbe, david sanger photography, Danita
Delimont, Mitchell Funk, Roberto Soncin Gerometta, Dennis Hallinan, The Hoberman Collection,
ImageState, Andrew Jankunas, Bjanka Kadic, Art Kowalsky, Ron Niebrugge, PHOTOTAKE Inc., Steven Poe,
Profimedia.CZ.s.r.o., Robert Harding Picture Library Ltd, MARC ROMANELLI, vittorio sciosia,
SCPhotos, SHOTFILE, Stephen Saks Photography, Stock Connection, Stock Connection Distrobution,
Chris Sutton, Tom Tracy Photography, Weldon Thomson, Underwood Archives), Design Maps, Inc.,
Getty Images (Bill Derrick, Keystone, John Lamb)

Printed in the United States of America

Library of Congress Cataloging-in-Publication Data
Fandel, Jennifer.
Golden Gate Bridge / by Jennifer Fandel.
p. cm. — (Modern wonders of the world)
Includes index.
ISBN-13: 978-1-58341-437-8
1. Golden Gate Bridge (San Francisco, Calif.)—Juvenile literature. I. Title. II. Series.

TG25.S225.G36 2006   624.2'30979461—dc22   2005037233

First edition

2 4 6 8 9 7 5 3 1

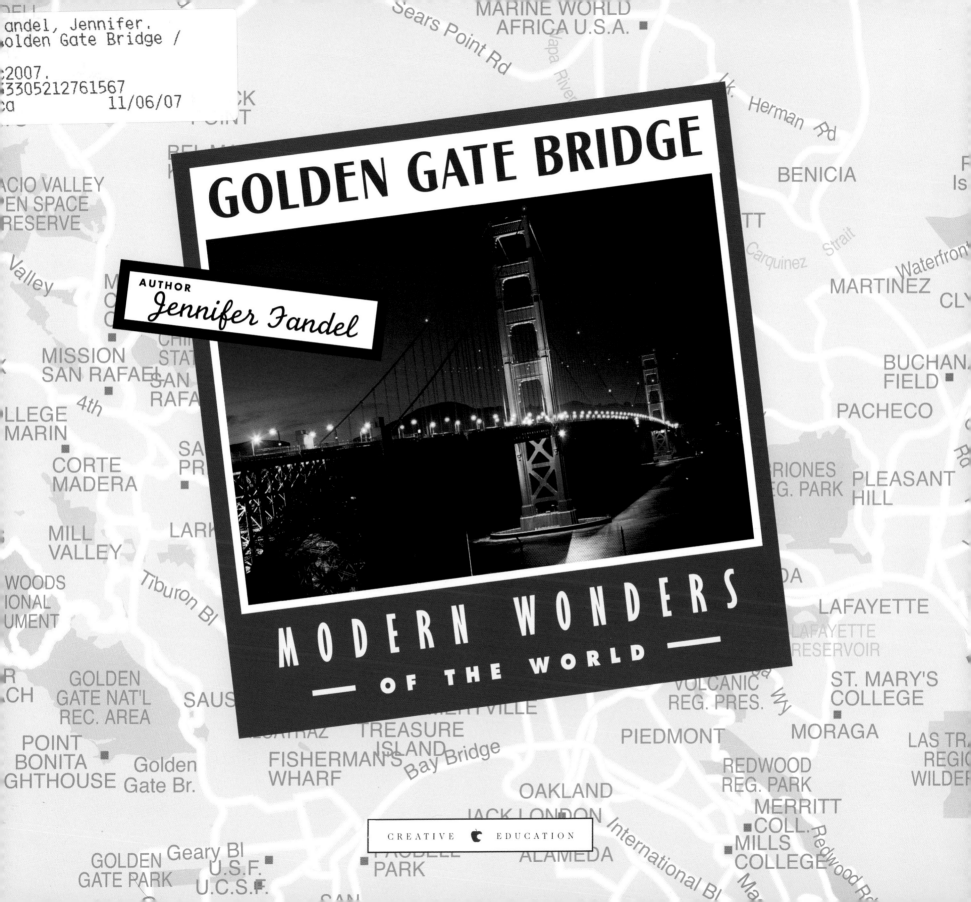

GOLDEN GATE BRIDGE

AUTHOR
Jennifer Fandel

MODERN WONDERS
OF THE WORLD

CREATIVE ☀ EDUCATION

GOLDEN GATE  BRIDGE

The immense span of the Golden Gate Bridge inspires awe whether viewed from a car atop its roadway, a ship about to pass under its deck, or an airplane circling high above its towers.

No matter if it is under clear blue skies or is shrouded in fog, the Golden Gate Bridge's bright orange form takes hold of the San Francisco skyline and commands attention. Welcoming travelers to America's western shore, the Golden Gate Bridge is the most recognizable bridge in the world. At the time it was built, no one believed a bridge could span such a distance and withstand the area's raging winds, high tides, and earthquakes. But more than six decades later, the landmark continues to stand firm. Imagining the San Francisco skyline without the Golden Gate Bridge seems impossible, for the graceful structure has come to represent the city and its dreams.

BRIDGING THE DISTANCE

Joseph B. Strauss, the Golden Gate Bridge's chief engineer, was a small man—little more than five feet (1.5 m) tall—who dreamed of building big things. For his final college project, he designed a bridge to be built across the Bering Strait, the waterway separating Russia from North America. It was never built.

San Francisco, California, is a city of water. To the west, the Pacific Ocean stretches into the horizon. To the east is the San Francisco Bay, a large natural harbor for ocean-going ships. The Golden Gate, a one-mile-wide (1.6 km) **strait** connecting these two bodies of water, separates San Francisco from California counties to the north. Because of the strait's rough waters and dangerous storms, people believed for decades that bridging it was impossible. The notion wasn't given serious consideration until 1917, when an engineer named Joseph B. Strauss put forward the first design for a bridge across the Golden Gate.

In the 1920s, the popularity of the recently invented automobile changed the American way of life. More and more automobiles filled the roadways, and as the vast country seemed to get smaller, cities began to expand and increase in population. San Francisco, built on a **peninsula**, had no place to grow. Some city-dwellers moved to the rural counties across the Golden Gate, and soon **suburbs** began to develop. Many suburbanites traveled south across the strait by **ferry** to jobs in San Francisco each day.

The 1920s were a wild, exciting decade, and Americans with wealth wanted to spend it, entertaining themselves with expensive

Today, record numbers of cars travel America's roadways, making the Golden Gate Bridge more vital than ever. Although ferries still carry people across the Golden Gate, more than 100,000 cars pass over the bridge each day, making the structure practically glow during the evening rush hour.

John C. Fremont, a surveyor and engineer for the U.S. Army, gave the Golden Gate its name in 1846. The strait reminded him of a harbor in Istanbul, Turkey, called the Golden Horn. The name "Golden Gate" became popularized a few years later when California became a gold rush hotspot.

The Golden Gate has long been known for its fog, which today often billows up around the Golden Gate Bridge, making it appear to float in midair.

parties, elegant clothes, luxury automobiles, and vacations. On weekends, many took brief trips to the countryside to escape the bustle of the city. Many people living in San Francisco enjoyed traveling to northern California, known for its rugged Pacific coastline, beautiful beaches, and enormous redwood trees. The ferries, however, couldn't keep up with the demand. People waited in traffic for hours to board the ferries, hoping that the rumored plans to "bridge the Gate" were really true.

Throughout the 1920s, Strauss gradually gained support for a bridge across the Golden Gate by meeting with citizens of San Francisco and the counties to the north. In 1929, however, he encountered an unforeseen obstacle. The **stock market** suddenly crashed, sending the U.S. into the **Great Depression**. Throughout the nation, people lost their jobs, and businesses closed their doors. The government, struggling to keep the country afloat, turned down Strauss's request for funding.

In spite of these economic hardships, residents of San Francisco and five counties to its north raised the $35 million estimated as the cost of the bridge through **bonds**. Because building a bridge across the Golden Gate would supply the area with more jobs, locals were willing to pay for the project in order to see San Francisco thrive again.

8

Gold was the color originally planned for the bridge. The U.S. Navy wanted the bridge painted yellow with black stripes to help ships spot it through fog. Eventually, architect Irving Morrow selected a color known as International Orange, which harmonized with the sky, fog, and surrounding land.

In 1933, when the bridge-building project began, men from around the country flocked to the worksite, hoping to be one of the lucky ones selected for a job. Although President Franklin D. Roosevelt's **New Deal** program created jobs for many people, millions throughout the United States were still unemployed. To men with families to feed, the considerable danger of the work didn't matter. Over the next four years, the workers doing the diving, riveting, and cabling would endure some of the worst conditions imaginable—high winds, roaring tides, blinding fog, and chilling rain—to raise the enormous bridge into the San Francisco skyline.

In the early 1900s, growing populations and improved transportation around the world made bridge-building a universal dream. Improvements in bridge technology—especially the use of steel and cement—helped engineers build bridges that were stronger, longer, and more durable than earlier structures of wood, stone, and iron. While many new bridges were being built at this time, few generated the excitement that accompanied the Golden Gate Bridge. At a time of hardship, the bridge gave people hope for a more prosperous America. It united people in a common effort—to build a great bridge as a monument to a better tomorrow.

The International Orange paint of the Golden Gate Bridge not only complements the structure's natural setting; the bright color also makes the bridge visible to ships below. In addition, the paint protects the bridge's steel components from rusting in the ocean air.

CONSTRUCTING THE IMPOSSIBLE

The work and worry of such an enormous project affected the health of the bridge's chief engineer. Joseph B. Strauss died of a stroke at age 68, only a year after the bridge's opening. Today, a statue of him stands near the bridge. Its dedication reads simply: "The Man Who Built the Bridge."

Joseph Strauss's main concern was for his workers, who—like maintenance workers today (right)—often found themselves nearly 75 stories above the water.

The Pacific Ocean brings fierce storms, rough waters, and high winds into the Golden Gate. Additionally, the area is an earthquake zone. By the early 1900s, scientists had determined that rigid bridges could fracture and collapse in such conditions. Joseph Strauss and his two engineering consultants, Charles Ellis and Leon Moisseiff, determined that a suspension bridge would be the best fit for the Golden Gate.

In the 1930s, when work began on the Golden Gate Bridge, suspension bridges were becoming more common. In earlier bridge designs, the main supports were normally beneath the roadway, holding it up. The roadway in a suspension bridge is suspended, or hung, from strong

wire cables. The cables are flexible, allowing the bridge to expand and contract in hot and cold weather and to swing in high winds without breaking.

The project got underway in January 1933 as workers dynamited rocks and dug pits for the bridge's anchorages. The anchorages, made of thick cement, hold the ends of the giant cables at opposite shores, "anchoring" the bridge to the ground. Finished a month later, this first task was quite simple compared to the monumental steps that lay ahead.

The Golden Gate Bridge broke new ground in the history of bridge design. Never before had a bridge been attempted at an ocean entrance, and the building project was

Today, the Golden Gate Bridge provides a constant backdrop for San Francisco's coastal activities, from wading (opposite top) to golfing (opposite bottom). The workers who built this dramatic structure faced perilous conditions as they worked to span the 400-foot-deep (130 m) Golden Gate (right).

dangerous, expensive, and time-consuming. Workers easily constructed the concrete north pier, the cement pillar on which the north tower would rest, by June 1933. The south pier, however, was to be built 100 feet (30.5 m) below the surface waters of the rough Pacific Ocean. This required the work of divers and the construction of a huge protective concrete barrier, called a fender, around the pier. The south pier took nearly a year and a half to complete.

Meanwhile, the two towers of the bridge, supported by the piers, were constructed out of preformed steel pieces. For two years, workers riveted the steel pieces together from the piers upward, until the structures reached into the sky. The workers and their foremen took increased precautions as they climbed higher. Hard hats were required for all jobs, and a huge safety net was strung beneath the bridge. At that time in bridge construction, one life was typically lost for every $1 million spent. While 10 workers lost their lives in falls from the Golden Gate Bridge's wet, slippery steel, the net saved 19 others.

After completion of the gigantic towers, workers spun the main cables between the towers and down to the anchorages. First, to reach the opposite tower, they created rough footbridges of wire rope and wooden planks.

San Francisco sits on 47 square miles (76 sq km) of land almost completely surrounded by water. Even though it is one of the United States' most densely populated cities, with more than 750,000 people, another 125,000 people commute to the city to work each day.

In just over four years, the Golden Gate Bridge, once deemed impossible, became a reality. Upon its completion, the bridge immediately became San Francisco's most renowned landmark. An excellent maintenance program keeps the structure looking as new today as the day it opened.

Then, workers used a cabling machine to spin the wire between the towers. The main cable was created out of 27,000 pencil-thin wires bundled into 61 thick strands. The two main cables were more than three feet (.9 m) thick and featured 80,000 miles (128,720 km) of steel wire—enough to wind completely around Earth three times.

Next, workers pressed the wires together and wrapped them in a steel covering. Finally, smaller sus-pender cables were hung over the main cables. These smaller cables would be attached to the roadway, keeping it suspended 220 feet (67 m) above the ocean waters. This height would allow ships to safely enter and exit the busy harbor. The nine-month cabling process was finished by May 1936.

For the next five months, workers built the steel-supported roadway. To keep the tension on the sus-pender cables equally dis-tributed, workers began at the towers, laying the steel deck in each direction. After completion of the deck, workers laid the pavement. On April 28, 1937, a worker fastened a pure gold rivet into the center span of the bridge, signaling the end of the construction.

A full-time crew of 17 ironworkers and 38 painters maintains the Golden Gate Bridge today. The ironworkers repair the corroding steel and rivets, while the painters constantly touch up the paint. Their mobile scaffolding contains a toilet since it's so time-consuming to reach their worksite each day.

A MODERN WONDER

San Francisco's foggy season lasts from July through October. During those months, the Golden Gate Bridge's foghorns may sound for more than five hours a day to give warning to incoming ships. During the rest of the year, they can be heard between two and three hours a day.

The same wind that powers the yachts (opposite) sailing the Golden Gate can cause the roadway of suspension bridges to roll violently (right).

Never before in history had people thrown a week-long party for a bridge. On May 27, 1937, the day the Golden Gate Bridge was opened to the world, 200,000 people arrived to walk across the bridge. But that's not all they did. People ate picnic lunches. They juggled, skated, and danced. Some even carved their names into the fresh, shiny orange paint. Now the West Coast had its landmark, just as the East Coast had the Statue of Liberty.

The Golden Gate Bridge, at its completion, rewrote all record books. Surpassing records previously held by New York's Brooklyn Bridge, the Golden Gate Bridge

became the world's longest and tallest suspension structure, with its **main span** extending 4,200 feet (1,280 m) and its towers reaching 746 feet (227 m) into the sky. For San Francisco residents, as well as bridge aficionados around the world, this achievement was something to celebrate.

Since its opening, natural events have occasionally highlighted the potential danger of the Golden Gate Bridge. On December 1, 1951, after the bridge had been in use for 14 years, officials closed it for three hours due to high winds. The roadway of the bridge rolled in waves so big that people in cars lost sight of anyone in front of them. After this, the

In 1964, the Verrazano-Narrows Bridge in New York City took away the Golden Gate Bridge's claim as the world's longest suspension bridge. Currently, Japan's 6,532-foot (1,991 m) Akashi-Kaikyo Bridge holds that title. The Golden Gate Bridge now stands as the world's seventh-largest single-span suspension bridge.

Golden Gate Bridge's engineers ordered that the steel supports under the roadway be stiffened. The bridge has been closed to traffic only two other days in its history due to strong December winds.

In 1989, after the Loma Prieta Earthquake, which struck San Francisco and damaged the San Francisco-Oakland Bay Bridge, the Golden Gate Bridge underwent massive renovations to help it withstand an earthquake measuring 8.3 on the **Richter scale**. Another major repair was carried out quietly over 30 years beginning in 1965. Workers stripped and repainted the bridge to protect the steel from rusting in the salty ocean air.

The Golden Gate Bridge has been featured in many movies, often as part of dangerous or tense situations. In 1958, the bridge appeared in Alfred Hitchcock's famous film *Vertigo*, about a detective with a balance disorder made worse on great heights. The 1978 movie *Superman* included a scene featuring a school bus filled with children in danger on the bridge. In the 1985 movie *A View to a Kill*, the wind and height add extra drama as secret agent James Bond and an enemy fight on the Golden Gate Bridge.

Before the bridge's construction, residents of San Francisco and the counties to the north who had attended planning meetings

22

Numerous locations throughout San Francisco provide amazing views of the Golden Gate Bridge. Although never a record-breaker like the Golden Gate Bridge, the rustic stone bridge (opposite) on Stow Lake in Golden Gate Park offers tranquil relaxation in the middle of a bustling city.

The Golden Gate is one of the world's roughest waterways. Many northern California freshwater rivers and streams empty into the San Francisco Bay. Strong **currents** are created when these warmer waters meet the cold waters of the Pacific.

Alcatraz Island (right) sits isolated amid the Golden Gate's strong currents, which sea lions (below) easily navigate.

made clear that they wanted the bridge to reflect and enhance the natural beauty of the Golden Gate. People were pleased with architect Irving Morrow's color selection of International Orange and his **Art Deco** tower design. Considered by some to be the largest Art Deco sculpture in the world, Morrow's towers consist of sleek, angular shapes positioned like steps to catch the sun and draw viewers' eyes up toward the sky. These striking features, along with the bridge's vast size, continue to draw sightseers from far and wide to the Golden Gate Bridge today.

The Golden Gate Bridge's grand design has awed and inspired onlookers since its creation nearly 70 years ago. At its construction, the bridge reflected the spirit of the times, providing inspiration for California citizens who came together in a common cause during the depths of the Great Depression. Later, for many American servicemen returning from World War II, the bridge became a welcoming symbol of their homeland. And today, the Golden Gate Bridge still stands boldly as the "Gateway to the Pacific" and a modern wonder of the world.

2 4

SEEING THE WONDER

In 1994, the American Society of Civil Engineers named the Golden Gate Bridge one of the Seven Wonders of the United States. The other structures to make the list were the Hoover Dam, the Interstate Highway System, the Kennedy Space Center, the Panama Canal, the Trans-Alaska Pipeline, and the World Trade Center.

An estimated nine million people from around the world visit the Golden Gate Bridge every year. Additionally, more than 41 million vehicles cross it annually. The majestic bridge has six lanes for traffic, and as of 2006, the **toll** charge was $5 for each vehicle driving into San Francisco (there is no charge for driving out of the city). Typically, visitors view the bridge at their own speed and in their own style. Some prefer to drive the bridge, while others prefer a slower-paced journey by bicycle or foot.

Pedestrians and bicyclists are welcome on the Golden Gate Bridge from 5:00 A.M. to 9:00 P.M. daily. During the summer, generally the busiest vacation time in San Francisco, the bridge can get very busy. Those wishing for a quieter visit should consider going in the early morning or late evening. Sturdy walking shoes are recommended for those who decide to walk the bridge's 1.7-mile (2.7 km) span.

Because of its location on the Pacific Ocean, San Francisco has a Mediterranean climate. This means that temperatures remain relatively constant throughout the year, even when other parts of California are extremely hot. Daytime temperatures in the winter average around 40 °F (4 °C); in the summer, around 75 °F (24 °C). However, because of the frequent storms that

While driving across the Golden Gate Bridge (opposite) is an extraordinary experience, visitors can choose to leave their car behind and rent a bike (left) for an even closer view of the magnificent structure. For the truly adventurous, surfing (far left) the waters beneath the bridge offers thrills of a different sort.

Throughout San Francisco, stunning natural views—of birds on a gazebo in Golden Gate Park (below), towering trees in the Golden Gate National Recreation Area (right), and the rolling hills of Marin County (opposite)—mingle with vistas of a modern city and the bridge that has brought it fame.

blow in from the ocean, the weather can change quickly. Strong winds, fog, and rain are never unusual for the Golden Gate Bridge, no matter the season. For this reason, tourists are advised to dress in layers. A windbreaker or raincoat is also recommended. Visitors should keep in mind, too, that the fog is greatest in the summer and fall, although it usually burns off around midday.

Many visitors to the bridge also take in nearby Golden Gate Park and the Golden Gate National Recreation Area. Golden Gate Park is known for its many gardens and museums. The Golden Gate National Recreation Area, one of the largest urban parks in the world and one of the nation's largest coastal preserves, stretches both north and south of the Golden Gate Bridge. Within its boundaries, visitors can see endangered plants and coastal redwood trees. California gray whales and sea lions may also be spotted along the coast. This unique mix of city and nature makes San Francisco a popular destination for travelers worldwide.

Famous San Francisco nature photographer Ansel Adams opposed the building of the Golden Gate Bridge. Fearing that it would spoil the natural beauty of the Golden Gate, Adams photographed the strait on numerous occasions in the 1930s to try to convince others of his view.

GOLDEN GATE  BRIDGE

QUICK FACTS

Location: California, between San Francisco and Marin County

Time of construction: January 1933 to May 1937

Opening date: May 27, 1937; it was celebrated with a week of festivities held throughout San Francisco

Composition: Concrete and steel

Engineers and designers: Joseph B. Strauss (principal engineer), Charles Ellis, Leon Moisseiff, and Irving Morrow

Work force involved: Exact laborer numbers are unknown; the project took a collective 25 million hours

Height: 746 feet (227 m) from the water's surface to the tops of the towers

Length: 6,450 feet (1,966 m), with the main span measuring 4,200 feet (1,280 m)

Width: 90 feet (27 m)

Cost to build: $27 million

Funded by: California citizens through the purchase of bonds

Nickname: Gateway to the Pacific

Visitors per year: ~ 9 million, not including daily commuters

GLOSSARY

Art Deco — a style of architecture and art popular in the 1920s and '30s characterized by bold, geometric shapes and swirling designs

bonds — certificates issued by a company or government that promise repayment of borrowed money with interest

currents — movements of water in a specific direction

ferry — a large boat that carries people and cars across a body of water on a regular basis

Great Depression — a time from 1929 to 1939 when there was widespread unemployment in the U.S. and a major drop-off in the production and sale of goods

main span — the length of roadway between a suspension bridge's two towers; it's also referred to as a single span

New Deal — a program begun by President Franklin D. Roosevelt in the Great Depression years of the 1930s to put unemployed Americans back to work

peninsula — a piece of land surrounded by water on three sides

Richter scale — a system for measuring the severity of an earthquake; a measurement of 9.0 indicates the most severe earthquake

stock market — a system of buying and selling stocks, or investments, in a company to make a profit; America's stock market crashed (dropped off suddenly) in 1929, causing the Great Depression

strait — a narrow waterway connecting two larger bodies of water

suburbs — towns or areas on the edges of a large city; many people live in suburbs to escape the traffic and crowding often found in cities

toll — a payment made for use of a bridge, tunnel, or roadway